CREEPY CRAWLIES COLOURING BOOK

COPYRIGHT PAUL McGRATH
2019

Instagram.com/paulmcgrath820/

LOUD LARVAE

CANNIBAL CRICKETS

EGREGIOUS ARACHNID

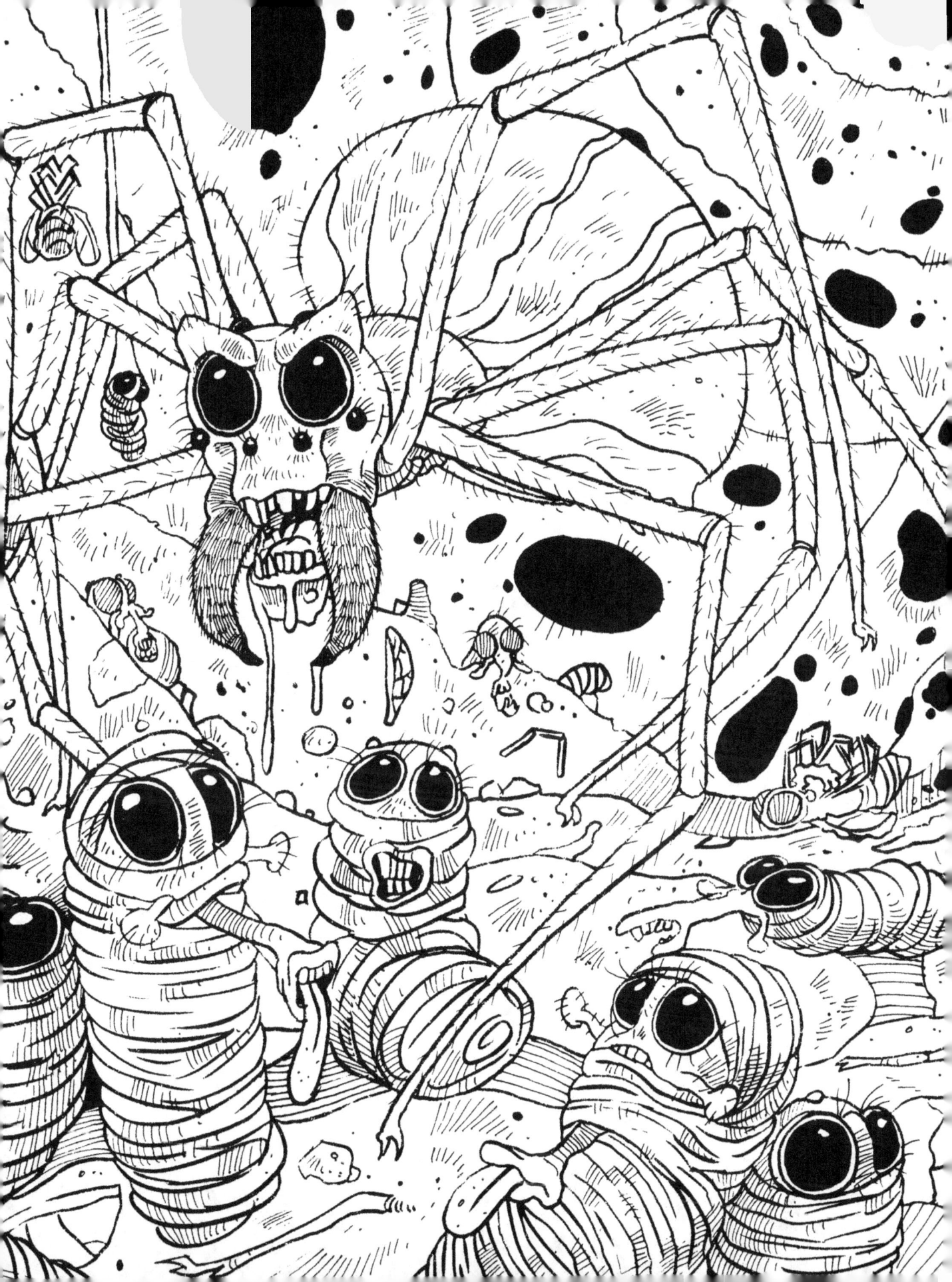

MACABRE MANTIS

SICKENING SCORPION

WRETCHED WOODLICE

BLASTER BOMBADIER

CRANKY COCOON

FREAKY FLIES

MANKY MAGGOTS

TANTRUMING TERMITES

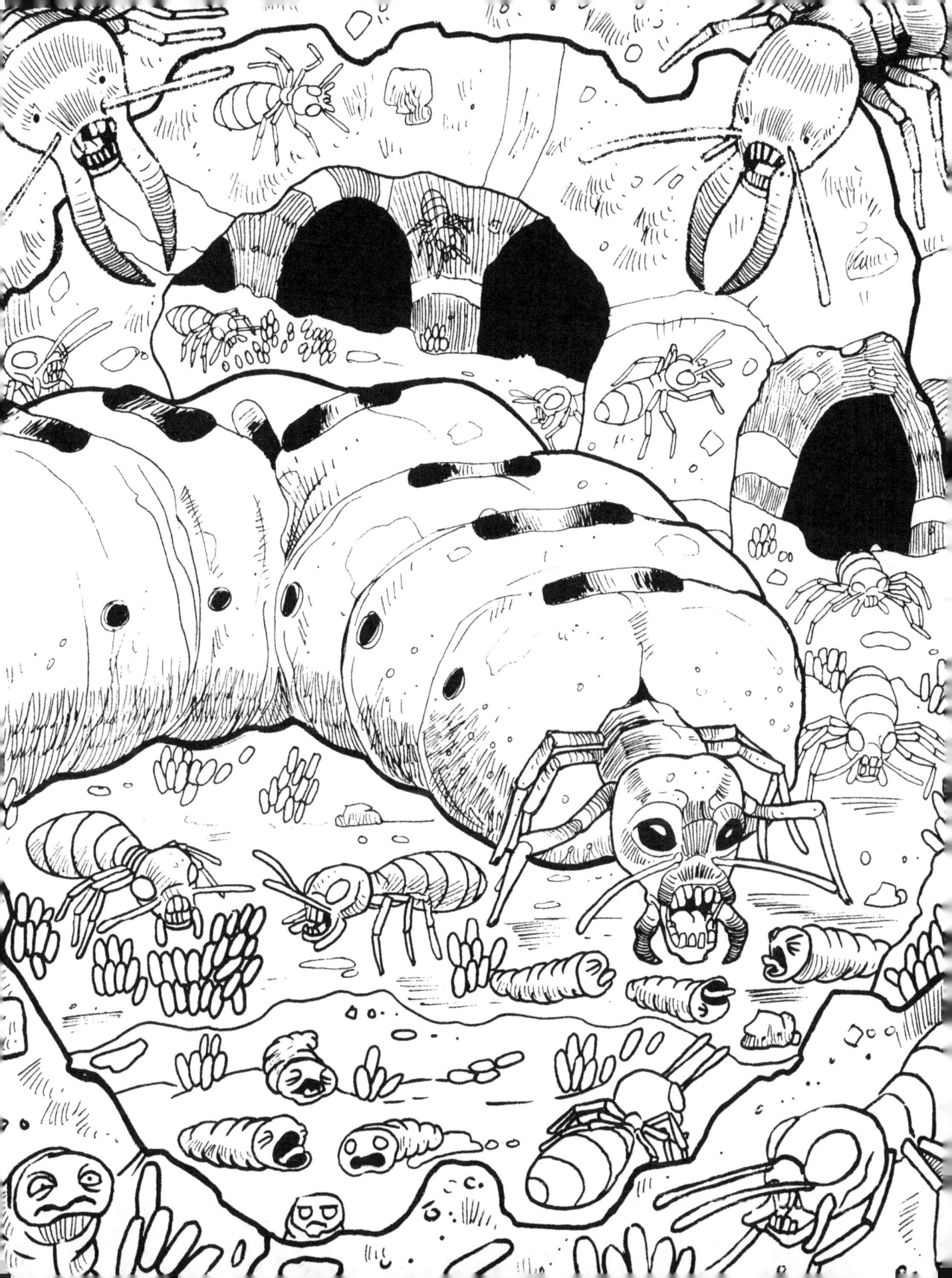

BOORISH BEETLES

CREEPY CRYSALIS

GLUTTONOUS GLOW WORM

MUSTY MOTH

BULBOUS BUTTERFLY

DARING DRAGONFLY

LETHAL LADYBIRDS

PETULANT PUPAE

WICKED WASP

CANKEROUS CATERPILLAR

DIRTY DUST MITE

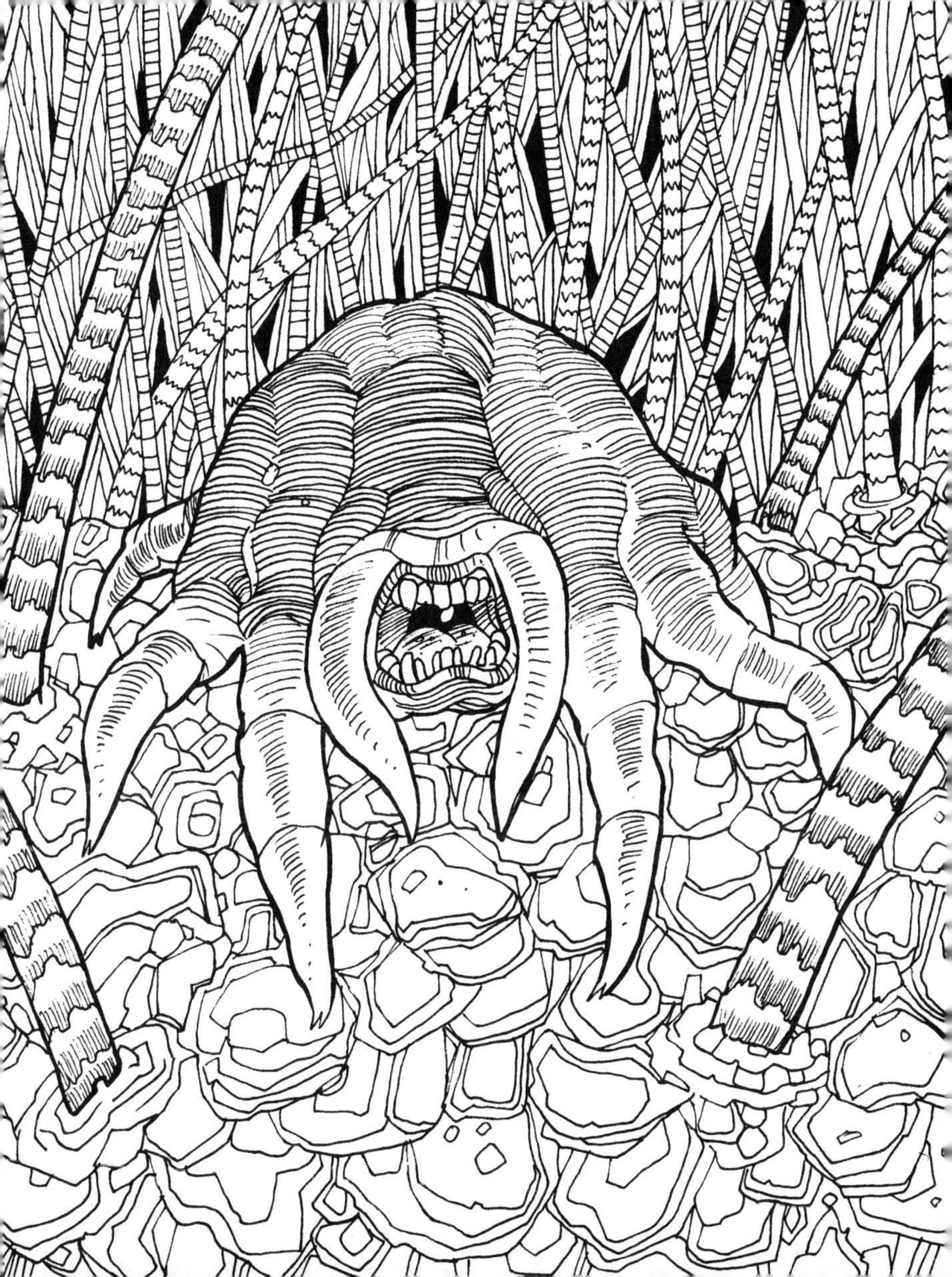

AFFLICTED ANTS

SICK CENTIPEDE

WONKY WEEVILS